Wisdom.
the Spirit's Gift

Christopher Cocksworth

Principal, Ridley Hall, Cambridge

GROVE BOOKS LIMITED
RIDLEY HALL RD CAMBRIDGE CB3 9HU

Contents

1   Introduction 3

2   Solomon's Prayer 5

3   The Jewish Wisdom Tradition 7

4   The Wisdom of Christ 11

5   Receiving Spiritual Wisdom 18

6   Making Wisdom Decisions 25

    Notes 28

Acknowledgments

I am grateful to the Leadership Team of New Wine for inviting me to lead some seminars at New Wine 2002 on *Spiritual Wisdom* and to those who came to them, to David Ford for two inspirational conversations and for his various writings about wisdom, to Rupert Charkham for pointing me to John Newton's account of his conversion, to students and staff of Ridley Hall who have been patient with me as I have spoken about wisdom and to the Grove Book's Renewal Group for encouraging me to write about the subject, with special thanks to Mark Cartledge and Mark Bonnington.

The Cover Illustration is by Peter Ashton

First Impression January 2003
ISSN 1470-8531
ISBN 1 85174 521 1

Introduction

1

'Where shall wisdom be found?' cried Job (28.20). He was in a desperate state. All that he thought he knew about life had fallen apart.

Job used to think that if you made every attempt to lead a good life, things would go well for you. But the apparent rewards of his 'good life' had collapsed around him. Wealth and health, family and fortune had been stripped from him. His friends had a raft of explanations for his plight, all of which Job found deeply unsatisfactory. 'Where shall wisdom be found?' he called out from the depths of this psychological and theological despair.

His ancient cry echoes through the Old Testament and it reverberates through the cultures and the centuries—'Where is the wisdom we have lost in our knowledge?' wrote T S Eliot in the twentieth century. Sometimes I search for wisdom in the Library of Cambridge University. Recently I discovered that the Library currently holds over seven million books and journals. If I was to read one book every day for the next forty years of my life I would have read only 14,600—that would be just 0.023% of the library's stock. When I told my children about this, one of them proudly told me that he was reading three pages of his book a night. I calculated that at that rate it would take him three and a half million years to read all the books in the University Library. Even then he would have another ninety-five smaller libraries in the University to work through. 'Where shall wisdom be found in these great libraries of learning?' 'Where is the data that is worth deciphering?'

Where is the wisdom we have lost in our knowledge?

From our kitchen window we can see the home of the brilliant Cambridge mathematician and remarkable human intellect, Stephen Hawking. As I see him making his way along the road in his electric wheelchair, I wonder, 'is that where wisdom is to be found—in the mind of that extraordinary man in that frail and failing body?'

Walking along the Royal Mile in the heart of Edinburgh recently, my eye caught a sign saying 'the Royal Road to Wisdom.' At first I thought it might be pointing to the great rooms at the top the street where the affairs of church and state are debated by Church of Scotland and by the Scottish Parliament. Nothing of the sort—it was advertising tarot card readings. Is that where wisdom is to be found—sold on the stalls of contemporary religion?

Apparently Socrates, the ancient Greek philosopher, would ask every new student seeking to join his school, 'Are you in love with wisdom?' Of course, this is what philosophy properly means, made up as it is of two Greek words *phileo* (I love) and *sophia* (wisdom). Proper philosophy, ancient and modern, seeks its own answer to Job's question, 'Where shall wisdom be found?' Job's answer, however, to his own question is theological—'the fear of the LORD is the beginning of wisdom' (28.28). As we shall see, the conviction of the Jewish wisdom tradition was that wisdom belongs to God, wisdom is given by God and wisdom is received by those with the right sort of response to God. One hundred years before Jesus was born this wisdom tradition had reached the sort of precision to declare that wisdom is a gift of the Spirit of God and that this gift needs to be prayed for:

> Who has learned your counsel,
>   unless you have given your wisdom
>   and sent your holy Spirit from on high?
>
> Therefore I prayed, and understanding was given:
>   I called on God and the spirit of wisdom came to me.
>
> (Wisdom of Solomon 9.17; 7.7)

We shall discover that the gift that the Spirit imparts as we pray this prayer in the name of Christ is more than a love of wisdom. It is the *wisdom of love*. It is wisdom from the 'depths of God,' given by the gifting of the Spirit in the community of faith, fulfilled in the way of love and finally manifested throughout all creation when all things are renewed in Christ and God is 'all in all' (1 Corinthians 2.10, 12-14, 13, 15.28).

Solomon's Prayer

1 Kings 3.3–38 tells the story of Solomon's prayer for wisdom and his exercise of a wisdom that was judged by those who witnessed it to be nothing less than the 'wisdom of God.'

Before it comes to Solomon's prayer, the story has some instructive things to say to us about Solomon's life. We are told that he 'loved the LORD.' He was a *lover of God*. His heart was given over to the LORD. We are told that he was 'walking in the statutes of David, his father.' He was a *follower of God*. His mind was steeped in the word of the LORD and his feet were seeking to walk in the ways of God. We are told that he 'was offering incense.' He was a *worshipper of God*. His spirit was honouring the LORD.

Solomon's prayer for wisdom was not an attempt to find an easy route to wisdom. It was a point along the road for a faithful servant of God.

Solomon's prayer for wisdom was not an attempt to find an easy route to wisdom

The story goes on to tell us that as Solomon was worshipping, the LORD appeared to him in a dream. In the dream Solomon acknowledges God's faithfulness and blessing to his father David and then recognizes the great responsibility that rests upon him, only 'a young lad.' He knows that he has been called to a ministry among and for God's people but he admits his inadequacy for the task.

This could be his great opportunity. There are aggressive neighbouring nations that need to be kept at bay. There is a magnificent temple that needs to be built. There is a nation to feed. Now Solomon could of course just feather his own nest. He could ask God for personal riches and popularity but he is a bigger person than that. Surely though, he is going to seize the moment and ask God to fulfil the promise given to David to make his kingdom an everlasting kingdom by giving to Solomon untold power and might.

All that Solomon asks for is understanding and discernment

Actually, all that Solomon asks for is understanding and discernment. He asks for wisdom:

> Give your servant therefore an understanding mind to govern your people, able to discern between good and evil.
>
> (1 Kings 3.9)

Solomon's prayer for wisdom delights the Lord who gives to him not only 'a wise and discerning mind' (3.12) but also blesses him with all those other good gifts that Solomon was ready to forgo for the pearl of great price.

Immediately after the dream we see a telling example of faithfulness and fulfilment. Solomon travels to Jerusalem—the seat of his reign—where he is to exercise his ministry as king. When he arrives he worships. He knows that his reign must be rooted in praise and intercession. Then he gives a feast for his servants. He knows he is blessed, and so he is going to live a life of blessing. Solomon went to the place where God wanted him to minister. He continued his pattern of worship of God and prayer for others. He lived generously. These are all signs of wisdom, signs that the gift for which he had prayed had been prayed for by one who was ready to receive the gift.

These are all signs that the gift for which he had prayed had been prayed for by one who was ready to receive the gift

And then the job begins—the ministry to which he has been called starts. It is not an invasion. It is not an economic crisis. It is not an intrigue at court. It is two poor and disadvantaged women each claiming to be the mother of the same child. It is grief and joy. It is the regular round of life and death. It is the ordinary affairs of human beings. But it requires extraordinary wisdom. It requires the wisdom not of Solomon but of God. And that is what Solomon was given. Solomon was able to discern which distraught mother was the true mother of this child.

> All Israel heard of the judgment that the king had rendered; and they stood in awe of the king, because they perceived that the wisdom of God was in him, to execute justice.
>
> (1 Kings 3. 28)

The Jewish Wisdom Tradition 3

The Jewish wisdom tradition[1] (which looked back to Solomon as its patron) is a body of thought and literature spanning a period from nine hundred years before Christ to one hundred years after Christ.

It ranges from profound insights into the nature and purpose of God (what we might call *theological wisdom*) to simple sayings about the most ordinary things of life—work, marriage, family, politics, business practices and so on (what we might call *practical wisdom*). Essentially the Jewish wisdom tradition seeks to answer two great questions: 'Who is God?' and 'How does God want us to live?'

We hear the repeated refrain: 'Get wisdom, get insight'

The wisdom tradition can be found in all sorts of places in the Old Testament. It is there in the Genesis creation stories, many of the Psalms and, of course, the accounts of Solomon's life. But it is concentrated in a number of books that are sometimes called the wisdom books of the Bible. In *Proverbs* we hear the repeated refrain: 'Get wisdom, get insight' (4.4), 'The beginning of wisdom is this: Get wisdom' (4.5), 'Be attentive to my wisdom' (5.1). Proverbs is the place to find out that every aspect of our living is of interest to God. In *Job* we wrestle with the deepest theological dilemmas such as why God allows the innocent to suffer. *Ecclesiastes* reminds us that life is a pretty empty, meaningless thing unless we 'fear God and keep his commandments' (12.13).

Proverbs is the place to find out that every aspect of our living is of interest to God

As we have seen, the wisdom tradition did not end when the last book of the Old Testament was written. It continued through the waiting period, the time between the Testaments, the long wait of about four hundred years as God's people reflected on his work among them and his word to them over the centuries and looked forward to the fulfilment of all God's promises to them. In this sacred space, this period when hope for the future was threatened by oppression and struggle in the present, God's people were yearning for wisdom. It was the age of the sage. And some of their sayings are recorded for us in two books that were very popular in Jesus' time and now form part of our Apocrypha—*Wisdom of Solomon* and *Wisdom of the Son of Sirach* (also known as *Ecclesiasticus*).

The Jewish wisdom tradition had a *relational* understanding of wisdom. It believed that wisdom was intimately related to God and, therefore, discernible in God's world and bestowed on God's people. We need to look at these features more closely.

Intimately Related to God

All the wisdom writers begin with the firm belief that wisdom comes from God (Job 12.13, Prov 2.6, Ecc 2.26). It is God's wisdom that we are called to seek and find. Some of the writers see God's wisdom as so important to God, so loved by God, so much used by God that they envisage wisdom in very personal terms, like a personal agency by which God works in the world:

> When [the LORD] established the heavens, I was there,
> when he drew a circle on the face of the deep,
> when he made firm the skies above,
> when he established the fountains of the deep,
> when he assigned to the sea its limit...
> when he marked out the foundations of the earth,
> then I was beside him, like a master worker,
> and I was daily his delight,
> rejoicing before him always,
> rejoicing in his inhabited world and delighting in the human race.
>   (Proverbs 8.27–31)

Hokmah, the Hebrew for wisdom, is a feminine word and often wisdom is depicted as a handmaid of God, a generous and gentle woman who invites us to a lavish feast (Proverbs 9.1–3). Indeed, the voice of *hokmah* finds clearest human expression in the wise woman, 'more precious than jewels,' who is the delight of her husband and the one whom his heart trusts and his life relies. (31.10–11).

Discernible in God's World

Because God created *through* wisdom (Prov. 3.19), wisdom can be found *in* creation. 'The earth is the LORD's and all that is in it; the world, and those who live in it' (Psalm 24.1). Accordingly, God has made a measure of wisdom available to all. 'To you, O people, I call, and my cry is to *all that live*' (Proverbs 8.4). The Jewish wisdom tradition had a big enough understanding of God to recognize that wisdom could be found in the nations (1 Kings 4.30) and was happy to draw on that wisdom where and when appropriate.

Bestowed on Israel

The people of Israel were able to hold this space for the universality of wisdom together with the conviction in the special endowment of wisdom within the covenant. They could believe at the same time in the immanent presence of wisdom in the creation created by God's wisdom and the transcendent gift of wisdom that came only through the redemptive relationship with God into which Israel had been invited by the grace of God's wisdom.

There were two things that convinced them that the depth of God's wisdom could only be found in the grace of the covenant. The first was the gift of the covenant—the Law. Through the Law God had revealed his will to the people of Israel.

> O, how I love your law:
> it is my meditation all day long.
> Your commandment makes me wiser than my enemies:
> for it is always with me.
>
> (Psalm 119.97)

The second was the condition of the covenant—the fear of the LORD. The people of Israel learnt that God required a fundamental orientation in life that acknowledged the lordship of God over life. They called it *the fear of the LORD*. It was not the *dread* of the LORD. It was an attitude of reverent awe before the holiness and otherness of God. It was respect of God as the source of life and giver of life and, therefore, the bestower of wisdom about how to lead life.

Although for the wisdom writers 'fear of the LORD' is proved by the fruit of a faithful life, Sirach the sage, writing in about 190 BCE, shows how it stems from encounter with the presence of God.

> The fear of the LORD is glory and exultation,
> and gladness and a crown of rejoicing.
> The fear of the LORD delights the heart,
> and gives gladness and joy and long life…
> To fear the LORD is fullness of wisdom;
> she inebriates mortals with her fruits;
> she fills their whole house with desirable goods,

and their storehouses with her produce.
The fear of the LORD is the crown of wisdom,
    making peace and perfect health to flourish.
She rained down knowledge and discerning comprehension,
    and she heightened the glory of those who held her fast.
To fear the LORD is the root of wisdom
    and her branches are long life.

(Sirach 1.11–12, 16–20)

This is the language of worship. This is the language of the outpouring of the Spirit of God in worship. This is where the fear of God begins, in the place of 'glory and exultation and rejoicing,' where the heart delights and the life of human beings is inebriated with the love and the joy of God.

The Limits of Wisdom

However, although Sirach and other writers in the Jewish wisdom tradition were confident that wisdom is available to those who fear and follow God, he remained cautious about the extent of that wisdom.

'Who has seen God and can describe him?
Or who can extol him as he is?'

(Sirach 43.31)

Sirach was a wise sage, he feared the LORD and followed the Law, but he knew much was hidden, much was unknown. He believed that God had revealed himself to the people of Israel but his plaintive cry 'Who has seen God?' shows that he had detected the weak link that could uncouple his religion. Like any good Jew he knew that there was a chasm between God and humanity that could not be crossed, a distance that could not be run, a fundamental difference that could not be overcome. How can we truly know who God is and what God is like if to see God is to die? How can we really worship God if all the time we are wondering whether God is actually different from the way we understand God to be? How can we have the wisdom of God when we are mere mortals and when God is the creator of all things?

But then there came another Jewish teacher about whom people 'were astounded and said, "Where did this man get his wisdom and deeds of power?"' (Matthew 13.54)—someone John's gospel was to call the 'Father's only Son, full of grace and truth' (John 1.14).

The Wisdom of Christ

We pick up the distinctively Christian story with Paul in 1 Corinthians 1 and 2.

In Corinth by the mid-first century the Jewish wisdom tradition had in many ways lost its bearings. It had parted company with both the spiritual dynamic and the religious caution of the earlier tradition. It had become strongly influenced by the Greek culture with its confident trust in human reasoning.

Gnosticism was very much in the air—the heresy that made *gnosis*, knowledge, the way of salvation, claiming that with the right techniques it was possible to become one of the privileged few with access to the riddles of the universe.

It was wisdom that broke the categories of human thinking with the extravagance of God's grace

Paul's missionary strategy in this city with its self-confident presumptions was 'to know nothing except Jesus Christ and him crucified' (1 Cor 2.2). He made no attempt to speak with 'persuasive words of wisdom' (1 Cor 2.4) in the style of Greek debaters. He wanted the Corinthians' faith to rest on the power of God (1 Cor 2.5) rather than on human eloquence. And yet Paul says that what he preached *was* wisdom. It was not the wisdom of the world but it was the wisdom of God. Strangely, in fact, it was the sort of wisdom that the Jews had been taught to expect. It was wisdom that came from God, transcendent wisdom, wisdom from above, wisdom that broke the categories of human thinking with the extravagance of God's grace. This was wisdom from the depths of God and it blew the human mind.

> God chose what is foolish in the world to shame the wise;
> God chose what is weak in the world to shame the strong;
> God chose what is low and despised in the world,
>   things that are not, to reduce to nothing the things that are,
>   so that no one might boast in the presence of God.
> (1 Corinthians 1.27–29)

Here was the fulfilment of what the Spirit of God had spoken through the prophet Jeremiah:

> Thus says the LORD:
> Do not let the wise boast in their wisdom,
>   do not let the mighty boast in their might,
>   do not let the wealthy boast in their wealth;
> but let those who boast boast in this,
>   that they understand and know me,
>   that I am the LORD;
> that I act with steadfast love, justice and righteousness in the earth,
>   for in these things I delight, says the LORD.
>
> (Jeremiah 9.23–24)

This is the way to understand and know the Lord—to see the steadfast love, justice and righteousness of God in the earth. Look at the man upon the tree, look at the weakness of the cross, look at the one who gives his life for you, bears your sins upon a broken body, look at this man and you will see God for this is 'the Lord of glory' (1 Cor 2.8). He is the wisdom of God. He is the truth of God. He is God suffering human death for us and for our salvation.

Paul says that this wisdom is too deep for us to grasp in the strength of our own minds. The capacity to grasp this sort of wisdom, the ability to discern this depth of God's life and heart and being, comes only as a gift from God communicated to us by God's Spirit. Only the Spirit of God, says Paul, 'comprehends what is truly God's' (1 Cor 2.11) and this Spirit of God, Paul says, has been given to us 'interpreting spiritual things to those who are spiritual' (1 Cor 2.14).

The wisdom to know that the death of a first century Palestinian Jew is the full and final revelation of the identity, nature and being of God only comes from the Spirit of God. The wisdom to know that the death of this person is the pivotal moment in God's redemption of the world, his bringing his purposes to completion and perfection, only comes through the Spirit of God. And the wisdom to live one's life and to die one's death according to the pattern of this saving death, comes only from the Spirit of God who leads us into the mind of Christ (1 Cor 2.16).

Essentially, therefore, for Paul Jesus Christ is the wisdom of God and the Holy Spirit is the one who leads us into Christ so that we have his mind and follow in his way. Jesus is the *content* of wisdom. In Jesus we see God—we see the source of wisdom, the one who is truly wise, we see wisdom. And in Jesus we see wisdom in action—we see God's will, God's plan to the bring the creation to perfection through Jesus Christ his Son. The Spirit is the *agent* of wisdom. The Spirit makes sense of Jesus and his cross and baptizes us into the saving life and death of Christ. And the Spirit gifts us to follow Christ and the way of his cross faithfully, leading us into the perspective, the view, the mind of Christ.

Jesus' Claims

Before going further with Paul's theology of wisdom we should pause for a moment to consider whether his claim that Christ is the wisdom of God is supported by the actual claims of Jesus as made known to us by the Gospel writers. Jesus' remarkable prayer in Matthew 11.25–27 and Luke 10.21–22 is a good place to turn for an insight into his understanding of wisdom.[2] Some time earlier Jesus had sent out seventy followers to heal the sick and proclaim the presence of the kingdom of God. They had returned with joy (Luke 10.17) and reported back to him how they had discovered that as they ministered in his name the kingdom had indeed become present and the powers of the enemy had been futile against them: 'Lord, in your name even the demons submit to us!' (Luke 10.17).

The Spirit was upon them through Jesus as they did what he did and taught what he taught

They had found that not only was the Spirit of the Lord upon Jesus to 'proclaim release to the captives and recovery of sight the blind, to let the oppressed go free' (Luke 4.18) but that the Spirit was upon them *through Jesus* as they did what he did and taught what he taught. This was a deepening of their confession of the Messiahship and Sonship they had already made (Luke 9.20, Matt. 16.16) as they observed Jesus' ministry. Now, through their participation in Jesus' ministry, their convictions about his identity as the Christ, the bringer of the kingdom and as the Son, the revealer of God, had been confirmed in their activity.

Luke tells us that:

> At that same hour Jesus rejoiced in the Holy Spirit and said, 'I thank you, Father, Lord of heaven and earth, because you have hidden these things from the wise and intelligent and have revealed them to infants; yes Father, for such was your gracious will. All things have been handed over to me by my Father; and no one knows who the Son is except the Father, or who the Father is except the Son and anyone to whom the Son chooses to reveal him.
> (Luke 10.21–22)

It seems that Luke is wanting us to see that Jesus' own insight into the significance of the mission of the seventy is revealed to him by the Spirit as he prays to the Father. He praises God that through sharing in his life and ministry, in his anointing, the disciples have been given the wisdom to see the true identity of Jesus as the Father's Son and the one through whom God's wisdom for the world is embodied and enacted in the world.[3]

Source of Salvation and Shape of the Saved Life

We must now return to Paul and remind ourselves that there are two main dimensions at work in Paul's understanding of wisdom. First, Christ and his cross is the *source of salvation*. This, in the foolishness and weakness of God, is the plan and means by which we are saved. Second, Christ and his cross is the *shape of the saved life*. The means by which we are saved is to be the pattern of the new life we are to live. Finally, in line with other voices in the New Testament, Paul is clear that both dimensions of wisdom are given by the Spirit to all (1 Cor 2.12–16, Luke 7.35, 35–50, John 16.12–14, James 1.5, 3.13–18).

> *The means by which we are saved is to be the pattern of the new life we are to live*

It is important that we have the bi-focal vision to see both dimensions of wisdom. It is all too easy for a person or a church to have received the first (that Christ and his cross is the source of salvation) but not the second (that Christ and his cross is the shape of the saved life). John Newton, the renowned eighteenth century Evangelical, is a good example.

Newton was in a terrible mess in his early life as a seaman and became an embittered, violent, hateful sort of person, corrupted by all sorts of unhealthy influences and cruel people. His conversion is a dramatic and fascinating story involving a prophetic dream in his childhood, a massive storm at sea in which he threw himself onto the mercy of God and a conviction that he would not be able to make sense of the Bible unless the Holy Spirit filled him. His conversion took place over time and he was the first to say that there was still much for him to learn but it was real nevertheless. Yet he still continued in his career of slave trading becoming the master of a ship regularly transporting slaves across the Atlantic. He knew the cross as his source of salvation but he had yet to learn that the cross defines the shape of the saved life and that the cross judged slavery and slave trading a despicable thing.[4]

> *He knew the cross as his salvation but had yet to learn that the cross defines the shape of the saved life*

The church at Corinth was an example of this at communal level. The church had been planted and grown because Paul and others had preached Christ and his cross. However, the shape of individual lives and the shape of the church as a whole was far from the shape of Christ and his cross. Just look at some of the issues that Paul has to deal with in the letter: divisions, lawsuits, sexual immorality, the necessity of care of 'weaker members,' disorderly celebrations of the Lord's Supper, chaotic conduct of worship and use of spiritual gifts. Individual members of the Corinthian church needed the wisdom of the cross given by the Spirit (spiritual wisdom) to live their lives in the grace of God faithfully and to minister the grace of God obediently. The leadership of the Corinthian church needed spiritual wisdom to guide and shape, care for and lead, nurture and grow the church according to the ways of Christ and his church.

Wisdom, Life and Ministry

Wisdom is deeply connected therefore with the character of the life we live and with the way we minister to each other and to the world. Wisdom about God, obedience to Christ and ministry in the gifting of the Spirit are three interdependent, interconnected fields of Christian identity. Each field interacts with the other at every level. Wisdom about God is learnt through faithful following of Christ and through the exercise of ministry in the Spirit. Obedience to Christ is shaped through deep Trinitarian and incarnational understandings about God and it is trained through ministering the love of God made known in Christ. Gifting in ministry is nurtured and grown as we discover more about the God who calls us into ministry and enter more deeply into the mind of the Christ in whose name we minister.

Wisdom is deeply connected with the character of the life we live

For some time now I have been telling those who arrive at theological college to train for ministry that they are here because *wisdom, obedience* and *gifting* have been discerned in them and that the role of their training is to deepen their wisdom, strengthen their obedience[5] and develop their gifting. I was encouraged, therefore, recently to hear Christian Schwarz, the dynamic Natural Church Growth specialist, speaking in similar terms of three necessary dimensions of ministry—wisdom about God, commitment to Christ and the power of the Spirit. He said that we all need wisdom to channel our commitment to Christ in the right way and wisdom to use the power God gives us for ministry in the right way. He used Colossians 1.9–11 to illustrate his point.[6]

Wisdom
[9]For this reason, since the day we heard it, we have not ceased praying for you and asking that you may be filled with the knowledge of God's will in all spiritual wisdom and understanding,

Commitment
[10]so that you may lead lives worthy of the Lord, fully pleasing him, as you bear fruit in every good work and as you grow in the knowledge of God.

Power
[11]May you be made strong with all the strength that comes from his glorious power...

What About the Gift of Wisdom in 1 Corinthians 12.8?

Before we move on to think about how we receive the wisdom that the Spirit gives to all who are in Christ, we need to spend some time considering the particular gift of wisdom that Paul mentions in 1 Cor 12.8 ('to one is given through the Spirit the utterance of wisdom')? To do so it will help to recap on some of our earlier conclusions.

In chapter three we saw how the Jewish wisdom tradition believed that God created the world through his wisdom and, therefore, that wisdom could be found in creation. In a measure, wisdom was available to all humanity. We also saw that the Jewish wisdom tradition believed that, by the grace of the covenant, the people of Israel had been given the gift of seeing God's wisdom with particular clarity and focus. In this chapter we have seen that for Paul (as well as for other NT writers) the wisdom of the world, even in the focussed form that had been given to the people of Israel, had been warped by the effects of human disobedience and by over-confident assumptions in the powers of fallen and flawed human rationality. According to Paul a new form of wisdom was needed—the wisdom of the new creation, the wisdom of God received and appropriated by us as new creatures, renewed in the image of God. This is what had been brought by Jesus. He embodied this wisdom and embeds it in us. The world has been created through Jesus, the wisdom of God and it has been redeemed, re-created by Jesus the wisdom of God. Finally we have seen that this wisdom of the new creation is cross-shaped and is given by the Spirit to the people of Christ who together make up the church.

There are at least three dimensions to godly wisdom. They include our *thought*, the way we think about God in the light of the cross as the people of

Christ. They extend to the pattern of our *lives*, the way we share cross-shaped life together as the people of Christ. They embrace our *ministry* and *mission*, the way we serve or minister the love of God demonstrated on the cross among us and the way we share with the world the love by which God gave up his beloved Son to the cross for the salvation of the world. And at the meeting point of these various dimensions is a Christ-like leadership of the church which seeks to discern wisdom for the work of the church.

I understand the gift of wisdom mentioned in 1 Cor 12.8 to be particular giftings or abilities that God gives to some members of the body of Christ by the Holy Spirit to discern the mind of Christ and so apply the wisdom of the cross to the thought, life, ministry and mission of the church in particular situations. This is very close to Peter Wagner's classic definition, in which he relates the gift of knowledge and wisdom very closely together:

> The gift of wisdom is the special ability that God gives to certain members of the Body of Christ to know the mind of the Holy Spirit in such a way as to receive insight into how given knowledge may be applied to specific needs arising in the Body of Christ.[7]

Wagner uses an analogy that helpfully illustrates the difference between the gift of knowledge and wisdom. He likens *knowledge* to the work of a medical researcher who has key and critical information and *wisdom* to the work of the doctor or surgeon who is able to diagnose the problem and apply the resources of medical science to treat the problem. Hence, the gift of knowledge may reveal the need for a greater degree of sacrificial giving in the church—and not just in monetary terms. Wisdom is needed to know how this can be preached and taught in ways that are consistent with the sacrificial giving of God. The gift of knowledge may uncover an adulterous relationship in the congregation. Wisdom is needed on how to handle and resolve that situation according to the judgment and reconciliation of the cross. The gift of knowledge may bring a picture, vision or word about a heart that is damaged. The gift of wisdom is needed to know what to do with that knowledge— how to minister with it, in the light of the love and healing of cross, discerning whether the word applies spiritually to the church or physically to an individual. The gift of knowledge may identify that the local Muslim community is feeling seriously threatened by the post-11th September attitudes to Islam and by fears of terrorism. Wisdom is needed to know how to reach out to local Muslims with the love and truth of Christ and his cross.

5 Receiving Spiritual Wisdom

The critical question, of course, is how we receive the wisdom that the Spirit gives. How do we take hold of the 'wisdom from above' (James 3.17) which the Spirit gives to all who ask for it (James 1.5)?

In true wisdom fashion, I would like us to make use of an unlikely source. It is a sermon preached in 1844 by James Garbett in Chichester Cathedral which I discovered hidden away in the rare books room of the massive library I mentioned earlier.

> And here, again, is the mighty difference between this and all other natural wisdom; that it purifies and masters the intellect through the heart, and not the heart through the intellect, as human speculators have ever dreamed, and do still dream. And the heart, which is thus made the true centre of all this wonderful compound, which we call human nature, is supernaturally changed by that Divine Spirit which cometh down from the Father, which is the purchase of the Son's blood, and which flows to us through the channels of grace which have been marvellously adapted to us, and framed expressly to convey it.[8]

As I sat surrounded by some of the largely forgotten wisdom of this world, I thought that Garbett had done a pretty good job describing how the wisdom of God comes to us. He says that true wisdom comes to us *as the mind is purified and perfected through the changing of our hearts by the work of the Spirit* (who is given to us by the Father and flows from the death of Christ) *through the means of grace.*

The prophecy of the Spirit through Ezekiel (36.26–27) tells us that God would give his people a new heart, a heart of flesh by placing his Spirit within them so that they would follow in his way. The prophecy through Jeremiah (31.31–34) tells us that God would place his law (his way) within his people, writing it on their hearts, so that they would truly *know* him. In the letter to the Ephesians we find this Spirit-inspired prayer:

> I pray that the God of our Lord Jesus Christ (the Father of glory) may give you:
>> a spirit of wisdom and revelation (as you come to know him), so that—
>>> with the *eyes of your hearts* enlightened,
>>>> you may know:
>>>>> what is the hope to which God has called you,
>>>>> what are the riches of his glorious inheritance among the saints
>>>>> what is the immeasurable greatness of power for us who believe (according to the working of his great power).
>
> (Ephesians 1.17–18)

True wisdom, spiritual wisdom, the wisdom of the cross comes to us as 'the eyes of our hearts are enlightened.' It is not about the size of our IQ or how many books we have read or how many degrees we have gained. It is about the changing and enlightening of our hearts.

The key question, therefore, is how the Spirit changes our hearts. How, for example, did Stephen become someone whom the Jerusalem church recognized to be 'full of the Spirit and of wisdom' (Acts 6.3)? Why could the Jerusalem Jews 'not withstand the wisdom and the Spirit with which he spoke' (Acts 6.10)? Paul gives us the big picture in Ephesians 3. Our hearts are changed as 'God strengthens us in our inner beings with power through his Spirit' and causes 'Christ to dwell in our hearts through faith as we are being rooted and grounded in love' (Ephesians 3.17).

Our hearts are changed as we are converted to Christ by the convicting work of the Spirit and then conformed to Christ by the transforming work of the Spirit.

Our hearts are changed as we are converted to Christ by the convicting work of the Spirit

But how does this actually happen? How does the Holy Spirit conform us to Christ and transform our lives into the life of Christ—the sort of transformative work that we see in Stephen who dies after the manner of Christ, forgiving his executors, filled with the Spirit, seeing a vision of Christ? This is where James Garbett's 'channels of grace' is very helpful. He simply points us to the means by which God, through Christ and by the Spirit acts to change us. Let us consider three main ways, means or channels of grace.

Worship (In Christ Through the Spirit)

Worship is a primary way through which the Holy Spirit strengthens our inner beings, Christ dwells in us more fully by faith and we are rooted and grounded in love. It is a primary way by which God leads us by the Spirit into the mind of Christ and forms wisdom in us because it confronts us with the reality of God as the God of love and the reality of ourselves as loved by God.

Worship involves facing[9] and touching God in praise, adoration, thanksgiving, penitence, intercession. It involves God facing and touching us through 'ministries of prayer' (forgiveness, blessing, prayer with laying on of hands and exercise of spiritual gifts), 'ministries of teaching' (reading of Scripture, preaching, testimony, prophecy) and 'through ministries of sacraments and signs' (water, oil, bread, wine, light, image, touch). Worship involves facing others and being touched by them as we join in the 'fellowship' (Act 2.42), use our 'manifestation of the Spirit for the common good' (1 Cor 12.7) and as we 'admonish one another in all wisdom' (Col 3.16).

Worship is a main means by which we may be led deeper into his ways of wisdom

Worship reproportions. It puts God in God's place (as the one who creates and redeems us) and us in our place (as created and redeemed by God). As we worship, the fundamental characteristics of God's relation with us and our relation with God become re-established and so the basic coordinates of wisdom are reset. Worship therefore is a main means by which God reorientates us to himself so that we may be led deeper into his ways of wisdom.

It happened to Daniel in a concentrated sort of way. He had been given a vision. He knew he needed wisdom to make sense of it. He placed himself in a channel of grace—*worship*. He fasted, wore sackcloth, marked himself with ashes, interceded, confessed and praised God. And as he was doing so he was given wisdom to understand the vision.

> While I was speaking, and was praying and confessing the sin of my people Israel, and presenting my supplication before the LORD my God on behalf of the holy mountain of my God—while I was speaking in prayer, the man Gabriel, whom I had seen before in a vision, came to me in swift flight at the time of the evening sacrifice. He came and said to me, 'Daniel, I have now come out to give you wisdom and understanding.'
>
> (Daniel 9.20–22)

In worship we learn the ways of God. Although this sort of learning instructs more than just our minds, it nevertheless has profound effects on our minds. In their study of the relationship between worship and theology Daniel Hardy and David Ford claim that 'knowing and praising God [are] intrinsic to each other':

> Our conclusion about the rationality of knowing and praising God is that in this movement not only is God known...but also God enhances our rational powers. By knowing the reality of God we are changed by it, not only morally but also rationally.[10]

God is 'the ultimate mind-stretcher.'[11] By knowing God in worship our rationality is expanded through the new horizons that God sets before us of the mystery of his love in Christ. Through the events and experiences of worship 'a loving rationality' (as Richard Foster calls it[12]) is formed in us as our understanding of how reality works is reshaped according to the divine logic of love. In worship, like Daniel, we become receptive to particular charisms of wisdom, moments when God speaks to us by the Spirit with intensity and specificity.

Living (In Christ Through the Spirit)

The mind of Christ is also formed in us as we seek to live in the Spirit, as we try to walk the way of Christ, as we make decisions in our daily living based on the characteristics of God's kingdom. Wisdom, like any gift of the Spirit, is not a static thing that we have and hold on to. It is dynamic and grows in the using. It is like a muscle that strengthens as it is exercised.

Wisdom is dynamic and grows in the using

Wisdom is exercised through discipleship, by our faithful following of Christ. I remember learning as a University Chaplain that the sort of preachers who made the most impact on enquiring but discerning young adult minds were, in fact, fairly elderly Christians, men and women whose faith had stood the test of time, people whose understanding of human life had been honed through years of dedicated discipleship.

The true test of discipleship is our willingness to take up the cross, to be obedient to the gospel in the face of suffering, to pay the price of following the costly demands of the cross and to exercise 'loving rationality' in our dealings with other human beings. St Francis of Assisi was absolutely committed to living out the cross in every aspect of his life and is a radical example of the sort of costly discipleship that is completely committed to living the gospel. In his dealings with people he showed an extraordinary, self-less wisdom that other people often found astonishing but strangely convincing. A formative moment came well before he heard God call him to 'rebuild the church.'

Sometime after his conversion he was praying and he heard God saying:

> All the things you used to love after the flesh and desired to have you must now hate and despise if you would do my will. If you begin to do this, the things which seemed sweet and delightful before will be bitter and intolerable to you. And those things which you used to shrink from will give you an immeasurable sweetness.

Encouraged by this word, Francis resumed his journey and very soon met a leper along the road. Leprosy in the medieval period was as much feared and hated as it was in biblical times and Francis had a particular loathing for the disease and its sufferers. But forcing himself to dismount, he gave the leper some money. Then, compelled by the love of Christ, Francis embraced the leper and kissed him. As he did so he found himself meeting Christ in the leper's touch. Radical following of the way of the cross became the mark of his life and ministry. From then on lepers became the special object of his compassion and Francis learnt that Christ is to be found by living in the way that Christ lived.

Christ is to be found by living in the way that Christ lived

Throughout his life Francis seems to have heard God telling him to do things which did not fit the wisdom of world or even the current wisdom of the church. They were the sort of apparently foolish things that made his own father distraught. You can almost hear him saying to Francis, 'Look I've given you every benefit in life including a good education and a professional training as a soldier and this is how you live your life.' The wisdom of the cross is foolishness to the world.[13]

Wisdom is also developed through study, primarily of Scripture but also of the deep seams of Christian wisdom through the centuries. Part of the answer to our earlier question about how God conformed the life of Stephen so closely to the life of Christ is undoubtedly that Stephen 'let the word of Christ dwell in [him] richly' (Col 3.16). Stephen's sermon before the High Priest proved that he was saturated in Scripture and guided by the Spirit to interpret the words of Scripture according to the gospel of Christ. He works his way through the scriptural story of Israel, often actually quoting biblical passages as he goes, and is able to show how it is part of the bigger story of the history of Christ. Clearly there must have been a powerful and particular work of the Spirit in and through Stephen as he stood before the high priest to confess his faith in Christ (Luke 21.15), but it was a work that was built upon his consistent study of Scripture, a study that had imprinted the character of God and the characteristics of Israel's walk with God firmly on his mind.

Their spiritual antennae had been tuned by obedient following of Christ and listening to him

When Bede, the historian of the early centuries of the faith in Britain, described the early influences of Cuthbert, the charismatic Celtic monk and missionary bishop, he singled out the formative effect of Boisil, prior of the monastery of Melrose in the south of Scotland and 'a priest of great and prophetic spirit.' Bede tells us that 'Cuthbert humbly submitted himself to the direction of Boisil, who gave him instruction in the Scriptures and showed him an example of holy life.'[14] Cuthbert was ready to learn from Boisil because he saw that he was someone whose thinking and living had been shaped by faithful discipleship of Christ and committed attention to his word in Scripture. Here was someone who, in walking the way of Christ and hearing the word of Christ, had been trained by the mind of Christ and so could be trusted to know something of the wisdom of Christ. Like those about Francis, the stories of the Celtic monks are full of examples of extraordinary insight and discernment. They were able to receive particular wisdom for particular situations because their spiritual antennae had been tuned by obedient following of Christ and listening to him.

Ministering (In Christ Through the Spirit)

Another main way in which we grow into the wisdom of Christ is by doing the work of Christ. As we follow Christ's way and hear his word we are necessarily involved in his ministry. It is only as we minister the love of God demonstrated in the cross of Christ that we discover the logic and dynamic of love.

I learnt most about my own father when I worked alongside him, whether in the seemingly unending round of DIY jobs about the house or in occasional weeks earning some pocket money at his office in a firm of London lawyers. As I observed him, listened to his instructions, tentatively tried my hand at the task, waited for the inevitable advice on how I could improve what I was doing and then, finally, as he released me to do it myself, I came to know him in a much deeper way than I ever had before. I knew how he cut a piece of wood and how, if I tried to do it in the same way, it stood a decent chance of being straight. I knew how he treated other people at work, especially those at the wrong end of the hierarchy in old style London legal firms, and I discovered that if I showed that sort of respect to people they seemed to grow in self-esteem and confidence.

The orbit of Christian ministry is staggeringly large—from individuals to communities to nations to 'creation' itself. It involves ministries of *communication* from teaching to writing, preaching to powerpointing. It involves ministries of *compassion* from listening to counselling, prayer for healing to prayer for deliverance. It involves ministries of *church building* from evangelism, to nurturing disciples, to the planting, growing and nourishing of the church ministries. It involves ministries of *community engagement* from the most local and popular to the most international and controversial. All require wisdom.

Towards the end of his life, when he was preaching at a conference of clergy in 1787, John Newton described how at least one aspect of Christian ministry had become for him the litmus test of whether we have begun to acquire the wisdom of God:

> *He that winneth souls is wise.* May it be written upon my own heart while I live! May it be written upon all our hearts! Let the scholar, the philosopher, the politician settle their several claims to wisdom, among themselves; but may *this* wisdom be ours. The man that winneth souls is truly and emphatically wise.[15]

The love of Christ for the whole world and every part of it drove him to the cross. And as Bonhoeffer said, we are called to participate in Christ's encounter with the world.[16] Doing so is not only a test of our wisdom, it is a means of both growing in wisdom (as our pastoral judgment becomes more closely aligned to Christ's) and receiving words of wisdom (as the promise of Christ to give us 'words and a wisdom that none of [our] opponents will be able to withstand or contradict' (Luke 21.15) is fulfilled in us as we testify to him and with him in the world).

Making Wisdom Decisions 6

How can we better make 'wisdom decisions?' How can we can think, decide, judge wisely so that we can live wisely and minister wisely?

Fundamentally it involves an openness to the Spirit to lead us into the mind of Christ to know and do the Father's will. Practically, this means looking for wisdom in *creation*, wisdom in *community* and wisdom through *charismata* undergirded by an attentive listening for the wisdom of Scripture.

We saw how the Jewish wisdom tradition rejoiced in the creation of the world through the wisdom of God and we saw that the New Testament named this wisdom Jesus Christ. We should expect to find wisdom in the world, in all the good activities of human thought and life, in all the disciplines of human study and skills of human creativity. It is God's world, upheld by God's word and sustained by God's Spirit. Nevertheless, our listening to the world will always need to be discerning, realistic about the capacity of human beings to constrain and corrupt wisdom by the limited horizons of human thought and the reductionist effects of human sin. Miles Coverdale struck a good balance in the sixteenth century when he said:

> All manner of learning should be tasted in due season and measure, with good judgment and discretion, under the correction of Christ's doctrine; so that the wisdom of God be above all other, our best beloved, our dove, our sweetheart: which may not be touched, but with clean and washen hands, namely, with high pureness of mind and due reverence.[17]

Wisdom in Israel belonged to the community. It had been learnt by a nation seeking to live under the 'fear of the LORD.' Preserved and passed on by one generation, it was a living tradition appropriated, applied and added to in consistent ways as the centuries moved on. It formed a compendium of understanding that condensed the experience of the whole community for the benefit of every member of the community. Wisdom was even more democratized by the outpouring of the Spirit in the New Testament era. By virtue of the gift of the Spirit, all the believers were endowed with wisdom to know Christ as the source of their salvation, and with the promise of wisdom to shape their lives according to the pattern of Christ through worship, discipleship and ministry.

When looking for wisdom we are to listen carefully to others, both those we cannot see because of historical or geographical distance, and those among whom we live and move. The 'familiar friends' of our books, as Richard Baxter liked to call them, are vital sources of wisdom for the present age as we seek to become, as Karl Barth said, 'fellow students' of the mind of Christ with those who have gone before us in the faith. And those with whom we live, including those in our own Christian communities who are seeking to hear and to follow Christ in the same particularities of life that we face, are also sources of wisdom for us in the present. Leadership is often a case of listening to the various voices of wisdom in a community and beyond, allowing those voices to hear each other and then discerning, with others, what the Spirit is saying to the community as a whole.

We have seen that in the Jewish and Christian tradition, wisdom is seen as both immanent (among and within us) and transcendent (coming to us from beyond). We expect wisdom to be *present* and to *break in*, to be *formed in* people's minds through faithful living and for their minds to be *opened up* to new vistas of wisdom as we are led further into the wisdom of Christ's cross. There will be all sorts of evidence of wisdom in a Christian community and yet there may be times when new perspectives are given to particular people. This is the wisdom of the charismata, the charisms of Christ, the gifts of the Spirit. The wise believer, especially the wise leader, will seek after these sorts of inbreakings and unfoldings of wisdom from God that enable us to see situations with a surprising clarity and to make decisions that bear the stamp of the Spirit of Christ.

Attention to the wisdom of Scripture requires more than a search for texts that prove our views and disprove the views of others

Looking for wisdom in creation, community and through charismata requires us to listen continually to Scripture. This is not simply a case of scanning Scripture for propositions about God by which we can test every other claim for wisdom. Of course, there are propositions in Scripture—summary statements that condense the Bible's wisdom about God and the world that can be used responsibly as criteria of wisdom. But attention to the wisdom of Scripture requires more than a search for texts that prove our views and disprove the views of others. The power of Scripture lies in the way it *positions* us before God and *places* us in a new sort of world where the first are last and the last are first, where the captives are liberated and the dead have been known to rise. This strange world of Scripture is the world that Stephen inhabited and that provided the framework into which the Holy Spirit could speak and endow him with the wisdom to confess Christ before the false guardians of wisdom of his day, not only with his lips but with his life. Ultimately this wisdom is the wisdom of love, as Miles Coverdale, who spent hours translating Scripture, knew:

> When we know Christ and the secrets of his Scripture, we love him in such sort, that opening him unto another, we both take fruit of him ourselves; and if we have knowledge of other sciences, we use them all to his honour. For better is it to have less knowledge and more love, than much to know, and not to love.[18]

In Luke's gospel Jesus defines the wise person as the one who prays for the Holy Spirit (Luke 11.9–13). As we pray for the gift of the Spirit to lead us into the mind of Christ in particular situations, seeking 'wisdom from above' (James 3.17), the wisdom of the cross, we are invited to *watch* for wisdom in the world, in the community of faith and in our sense of the voice of the Spirit speaking to us through the exercise of the charismata of the Spirit. We are called to *weigh* all things by the wisdom of Scripture and then to *wait* for the Spirit-timed moment to speak and to act, to make known by word and deed that 'one greater than Solomon is here!' (Matt 12.42).

Notes

1　Good surveys of the Jewish wisdom tradition can be found in J Blenkinsopp, *Wisdom and Law in the Old Testament* (Oxford: OUP, 1983), R Davidson, *Wisdom and Worship* (London: SCM, 1990) and B Witherrington, *Jesus the Sage: The Pilgrimage of Wisdom* (Minneapolis: Fortress Press, 1994).

2　Helpful analyses of Jesus and wisdom can be found in Witherington, *Jesus the Sage*, J D G Dunn, 'Jesus: Teacher of Wisdom or Wisdom Incarnate' and S C Barton, 'Gospel Wisdom' in S C Barton (ed), *Where Shall Wisdom be Found?* (Edinburgh: T & T Clark, 1999). See also M Borg, *Jesus: A New Vision* (London: SPCK, 1993).

3　The Son's revelation of the Father is, of course, the deep theme of the Johannine tradition. Wisdom in John—given by the Spirit and leading us together into the truth of Christ—is worthy of a complete study in itself.

4　See 'Memoirs of John Newton' in R Cecil, *The Works of John Newton* (Edinburgh: Thomas Nelson, 1844) pp 3–66.

5　It is worth noting that Solomon's disobedience eventually undermined his gifting in wisdom (see 1 Kings 11).

6　See Christian A Schwarz, *The Three Colours of Ministry* (Winfield: International Centre for Leadership Development and Evangelism, 2001) pp 15–17.

7　Peter Wagner, *Your Spiritual Gifts Can Help Your Church Grow* (Bromiley: MARC Europe, 1985) p 220.

8　J Garbett, *The Sense, the Mind, and the Spirit: A Sermon Preached at the Cathedral of Chichester for National Schools* (London: Hatchard and Son, 1844) pp 21–22.

9　For a developed study of the metaphor of the face in worship, see D F Ford, *Self and Salvation* (Cambridge: CUP, 1999). See also C J Cocksworth, *Holy, Holy, Holy* (London: DLT, 1997) pp 123–146.

10　D W Hardy and D F Ford, *Jubilate: Theology in Praise* (London: DLT, 1984) pp 112–113.

11　*Jubilate*, p 114.

12　R Foster and J Bryan Smith (eds), *Devotional Classics* (London: Hodder and Stoughton, 2002) p 161.

13　For examples of Francis' Wisdom see S Clifford, *The Wisdom of St Francis and his Companions* (London: Sheldon Press, 1978).

14　Bede, *Ecclesiastical History of the English People* (London: SPCK, 1990), p 256.

15　J Newton, *The Best Wisdom: A Sermon Preached in the Parish Church of St Mary Woolnoth, 1787* (London: Buckland and Johnson, 1788) p 3.

16　D Bonhoeffer, *Ethics* (London: SCM, 1963) p 110.

17　M Coverdale, 'The Means to be used in Christian Warfare,' in G Pearson (ed) *Writings and Translations of Myles Coverdale* (Cambridge: Parker Society, 1844) p 449.

18　'Christian Warfare,' p 509.